Animal Helpers: Raptor Centers

by Jennifer Keats Curtis

with California Raptor Center, UC Davis School of Veterinary Medicine; Carolina Raptor Center; Raptor Rehabilitation of Kentucky; Rocky Mountain Raptor Program; The Raptor Center at the University of Minnesota; Tri-State Bird Rescue & Research; and Peter McGowan of the U.S. Fish and Wildlife Service

red-tailed hawk

Even the fiercest wild animals, like raptors, sometimes need human help.

Raptors—including owls, eagles, and hawks—are powerful birds of prey.

golden eagle

But even excellent hunters with keen eyesight, sharp talons, and strong beaks can break bones and damage their feathers. Fishing lines ensnare these tough birds. They get stuck in mud. They fly into windows. Sometimes these birds are poisoned or shot. Many are hit by cars. Sometimes raptors become so sick or injured that they cannot fly.

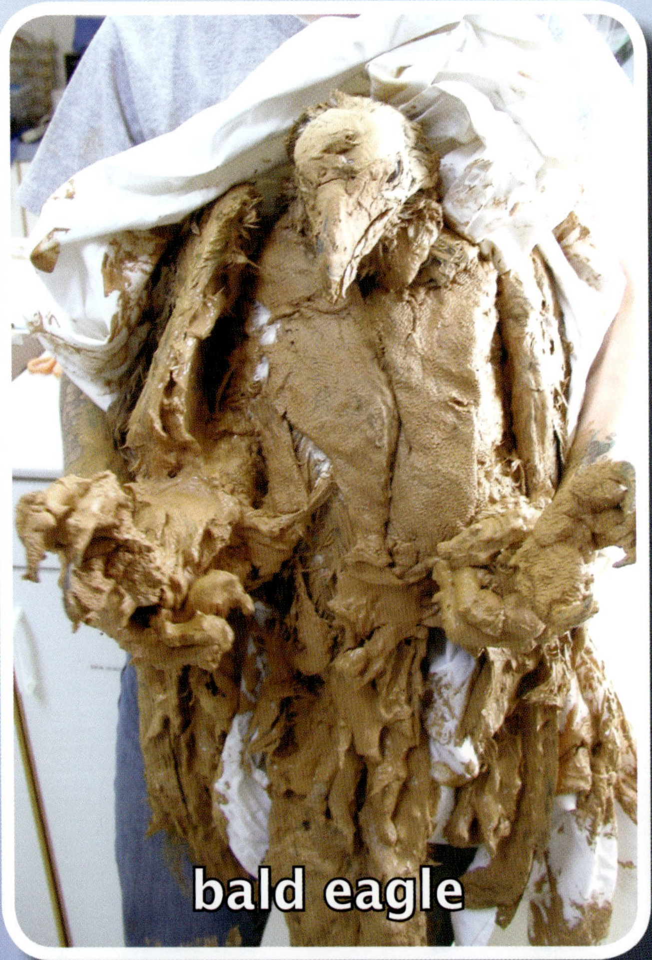
bald eagle

northern saw-whet owl

Baby raptors fall from nests or get blown out during storms. If their parents are not around, little chicks need help.

When these magnificent birds are injured, animal helpers in raptor centers come to their rescue.

If help is needed, volunteers rush the animals to the center or the experts go out to save them.

Just like in an emergency room, when a patient comes in, the staff evaluate her. Usually, it takes two people to carefully check the whole bird: eyes, beak, wings, body, tail, talons, and feathers.

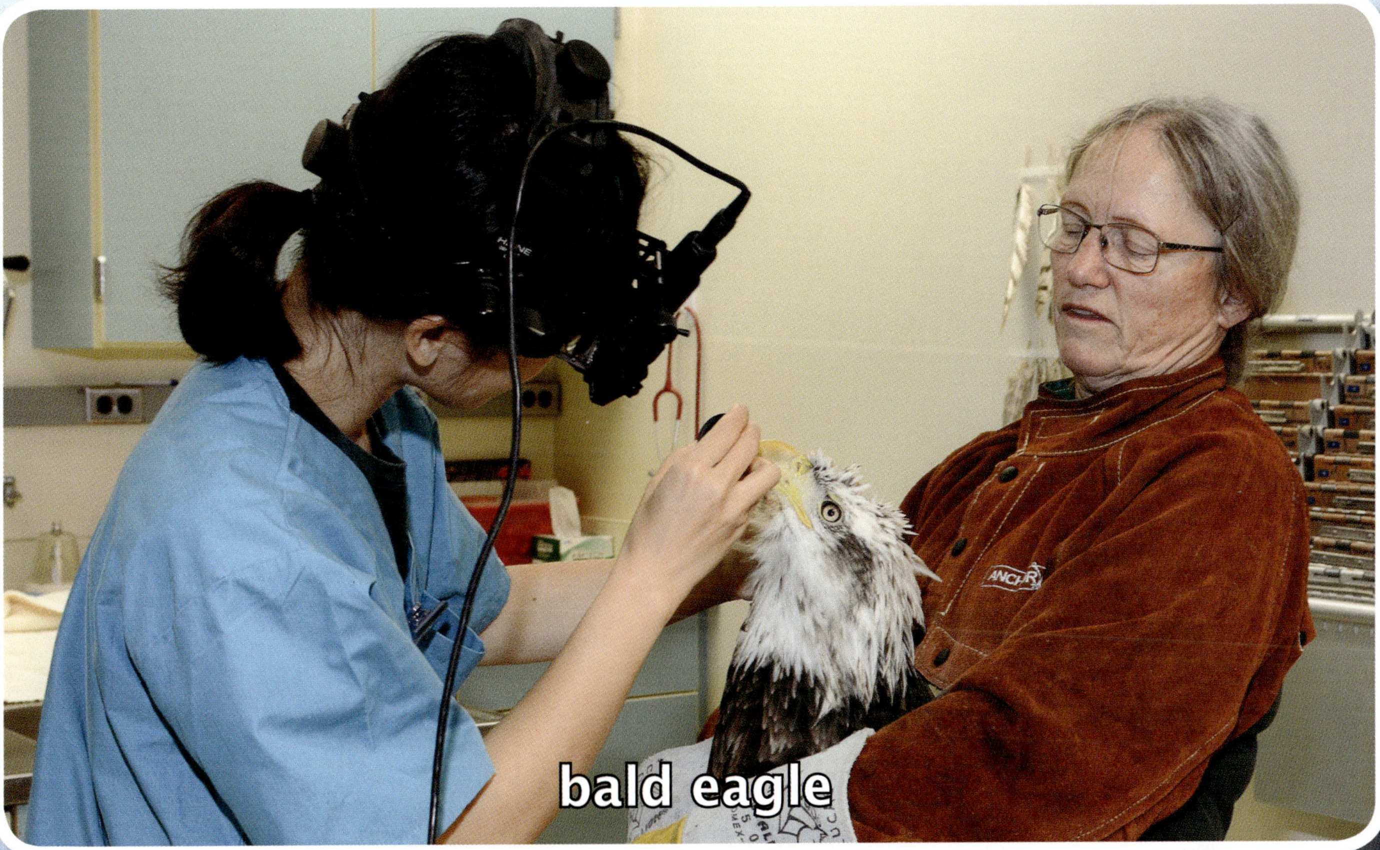

bald eagle

Of course, people are trying to help; but the raptor does not know that and may be scared.

great horned owl

Raptor center workers are part pediatrician and part detective. Like doctors of young children, these experts must look for clues to figure out why these birds are hurt and how to help them heal.

Helpers check for broken bones. They determine if a bird needs bandages or surgery. Birds coated in oil, dust, or mud must be thoroughly washed.

Raptor helpers decide if a bird needs medicine or just quiet and rest. If a raptor is ill, helpers might draw blood to find out why the bird is sick.

black vulture

Scopes help these experts look deep into the eyes of raptors hurt by cars or falls. Many raptors break wing bones. If a bird needs an x-ray, a hood is placed over his head. He breathes in gas that helps him sleep, much like how people are put to sleep before surgery.

If a bone is badly broken, surgery might be needed. During an operation, the veterinarian places a metal pin through the sleeping bird's bone to help it heal.

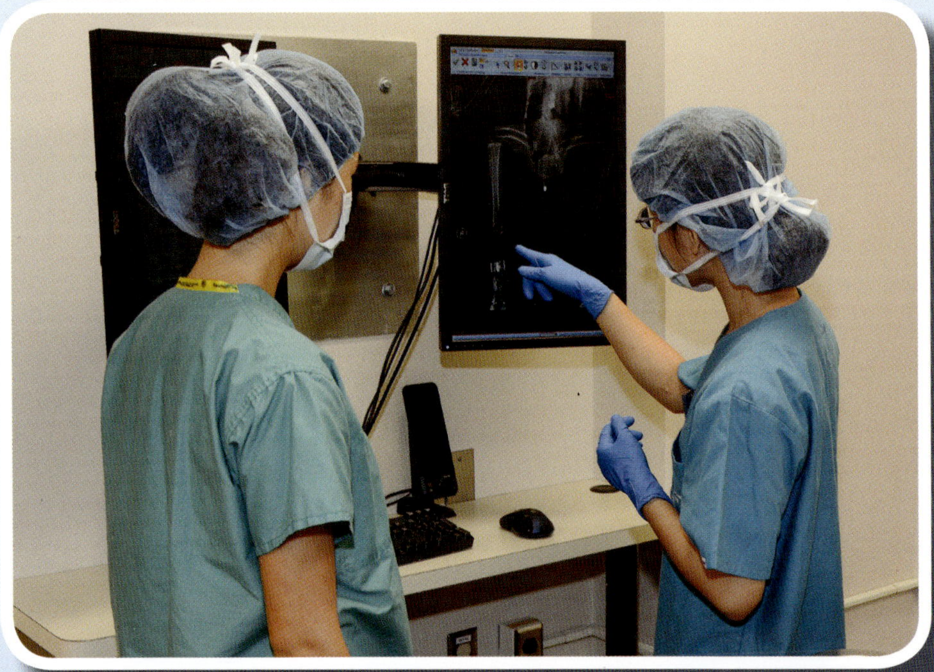

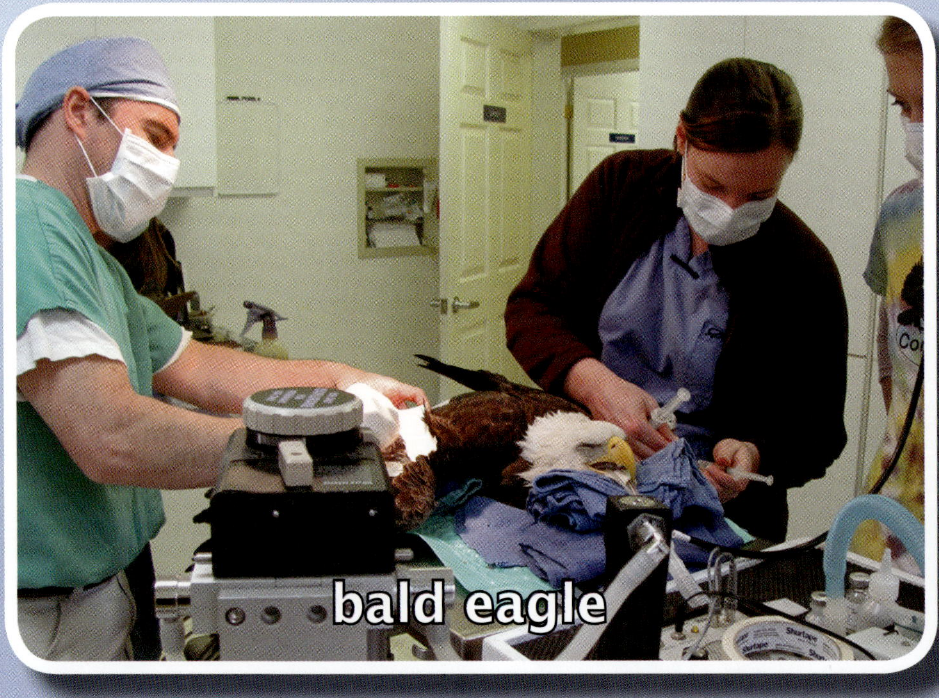

bald eagle

After surgery, the raptor stays inside the center. He recovers in a dark, quiet room. He might go into a small pet carrier so that he may rest. Or, his cage may be covered by a blanket to keep him relaxed. The helpers keep the birds in a quiet rehabilitation area to keep them calm and help them heal.

great horned owl

If the raptor does not need surgery, the bone is bandaged, casted, or splinted. It takes about two to six weeks for a broken bone to heal.

Helpers weigh their patients every day to monitor their growth. They give the birds medicine and food:

- grasshoppers for Mississippi kites
- mice for great horned owls
- beetles for American kestrels

great horned owl

Once the bandages come off, the bird might need physical therapy. Helpers stretch the hurt foot or wing. When the bird's broken bones are healed, he moves outside. It is time to practice flying again. He begins exercising his wings in a flight cage.

Within days, the raptor takes flight! Live food is placed in the cage. Helpers monitor him to make sure he can hunt.

barred owls

When babies arrive at the raptor center, helpers determine how old they are and how to help them.

Since the best place for young birds is in a nest with their parents, chicks are re-nested whenever possible.

osprey

northern harriers

If the nest or parents cannot be found, newly-hatched babies stay in the nursery. Helpers use tweezers to feed them meat and insects. In time, they will be big enough to join foster parents.

Foster parents, adults of the same species, readily accept the babies. As parents, they will teach their offspring to hunt, fly, and defend their territory.

great horned owls

Like their elders, young raptors must also learn to fly and to chase prey.

At some centers, when babies reach the brancher stage (about six weeks old), they are removed from the foster parents and taken to a nest box called a hack box. There, the young raptors become better flyers. They test their wings and begin hunting prey, such as the mice placed on or near the box. Within weeks, most have completed “flight school” and return to the wild.

red-tailed hawk

Since it takes time to become good hunters, human help may still be required. If necessary, helpers will put out food until, one day, the raptors fly away and become independent.

Many injured and orphaned birds are released. After weeks of healing, growing, exercising their wings, and learning or re-learning to hunt, they are ready to go back to the wild. At some centers, the birds are banded before they are released. With joy, raptor helpers take them to specific areas and let them go.

Despite the best care, some birds are unreleasable. They are unable to fly or feed themselves, or they are just too tame. When this happens, they stay at the raptor center or are placed in another licensed facility or education program.

red-tailed hawk

great horned owl

These birds learn to stand on a perch or a gloved fist and wear anklets, leather straps (jesses), and a leash to keep them from flying away or getting hurt. They serve as ambassadors—special birds who inspire people to learn more about raptors and the best ways to keep these species from future harm.

Would *you* like to work with raptors?

Could you feed mouse meat to a young red-tailed hawk?

Would you help hold a young bald eagle who needed her medicine?

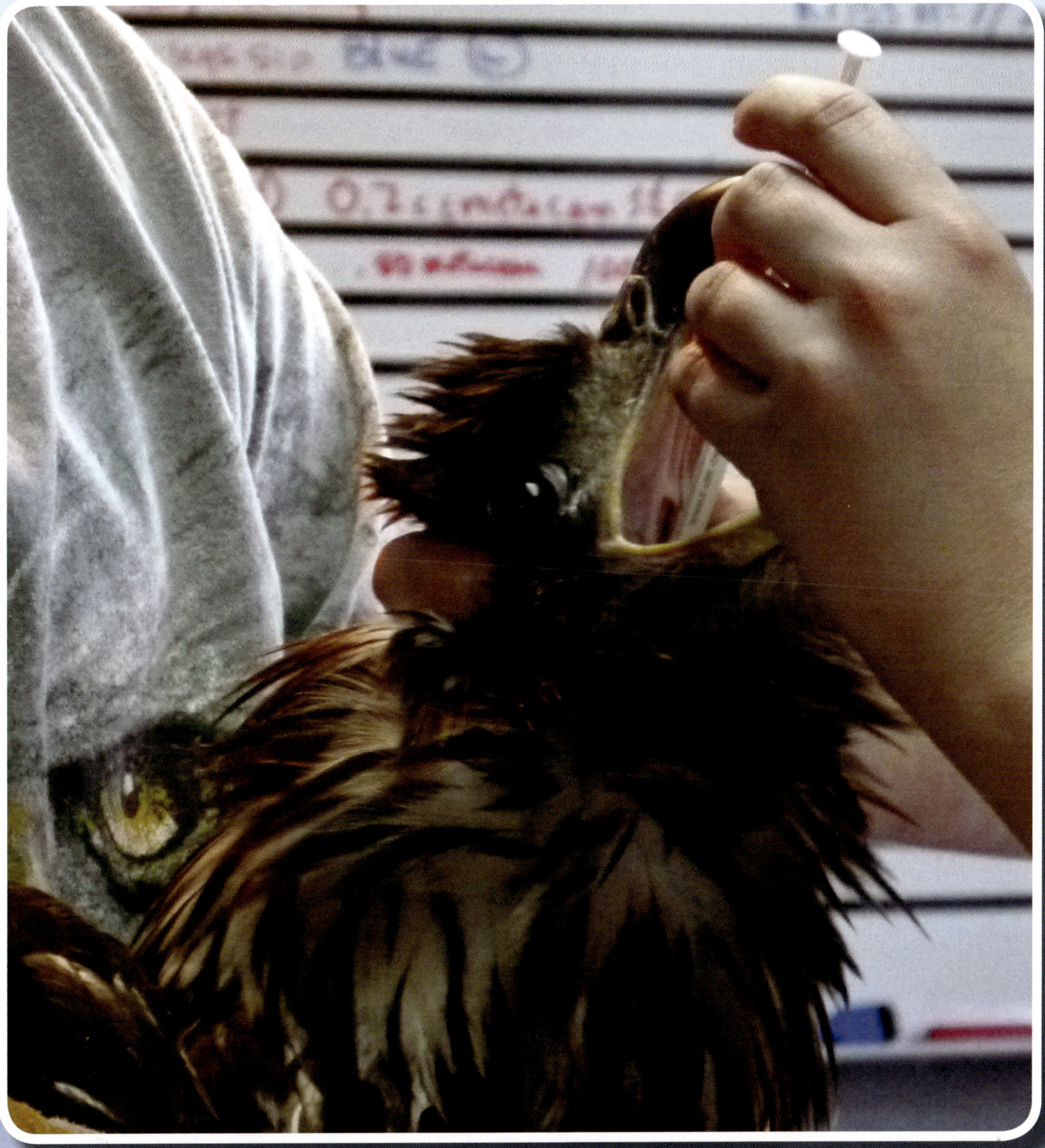

Could you weigh a newly-hatched great horned owl?

Would you clean the cage of an injured peregrine falcon?

Get to know some of these animals now! Read about raptors. Visit educational centers and raptor centers. Take a hike and look for raptors in the wild. When you get older, volunteer in a center. Your experience and work with experts will help you decide which animal helper job is best for you!

For Creative Minds

This For Creative Minds educational section contains activities to engage children in learning while making it fun at the same time. The activities build on the underlying subjects introduced in the story. While older children may be able to do these activities on their own, we encourage adults to work with the young children in their lives. Even if the adults have long forgotten or never learned this information, they can still work through the activities and be experts in their children's eyes! Exposure to these concepts at a young age helps to build a strong foundation for easier comprehension later in life. This section may be photocopied or printed from our website by the owner of this book for educational, non-commercial uses. Cross-curricular teaching activities for use at home or in the classroom, interactive quizzes, and more are available online. Go to www.ArbordalePublishing.com and click on the book's cover to explore all the links.

Diurnal or Nocturnal

Animals that are active during the day and asleep at night are diurnal. Animals that are active at night and asleep during the day are nocturnal. Read the following sentences and look for clues to determine if the raptor is diurnal or nocturnal.

The sun is high in the sky as the **American kestrel** perches on a telephone pole and watches for prey scurrying on the ground below.

These **eastern screech owls** wake up from a long day of sleep in their roost. As darkness falls, they prepare to hunt.

The **bald eagle** soars and hunts all day long before returning to roost for the night in the branches of a large tree.

One night the nest where these **northern harrier chicks** slept was damaged by farm machinery. Fortunately, a raptor center was there to help rehabilitate them!

After a long night of hunting, the **northern saw-whet owl** returns to her nest near a stream that runs through the forest.

In the afternoons, school groups and other visitors to the raptor center can see this **golden eagle** and learn more about his species.

Nocturnal: northern saw-whet owl, eastern screech owl
Diurnal: American kestrel, bald eagle, northern harrier chicks, golden eagle

Raptor Adaptations

Raptors are excellent hunters because of special adaptations that help them soar, swoop, see, and snag their prey.

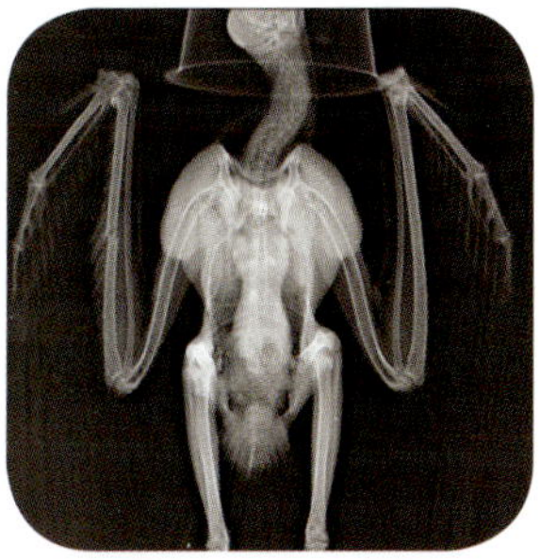

Like most other birds, raptors have nearly hollow bones. This x-ray of an injured raptor shows the dark, hollow spaces in the bones. Solid bones are heavy, but hollow bones are lighter and make flight easier for these birds. An adult bald eagle's wingspan is wider than an adult human is tall (5.9–7 feet or 1.8-2.3m). But even this very large bird weighs only as much as a human baby (10-14 pounds or 4.5-6.3kg).

Raptors soar through the sky on strong, powerful wings. They watch from high above the ground and wait to drop down on unsuspecting prey. The world's fastest animal is the peregrine falcon. When peregrine falcons dive to attack their prey, they can reach speeds of more than 200 miles (322km) per hour!

Sharp, hooked beaks help the raptor grab and hold onto their prey. Raptors can use their beak to tear their food into pieces or they can swallow their prey whole! Many prey animals have body parts that the raptor cannot digest, such as bones, fur, and claws. After a raptor eats their prey whole, these extra pieces form a pellet that the raptor spits up later.

If you have ever heard the phrases "eyes like a hawk" or "eagle eyes," you might already know that raptors have excellent vision. Raptors' eyesight is up to eight times better than a human's! An eagle can spot small prey the size of a vole or rabbit from more than a mile away.

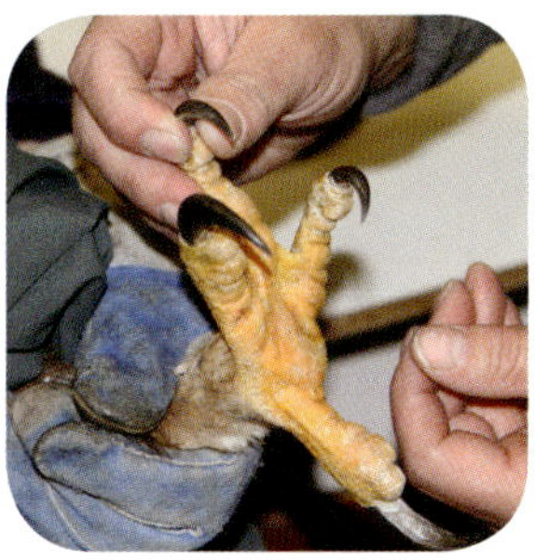

Raptors have sharp, curved talons on their feet that slice through skin and hold tight so that wiggly prey cannot escape. Owls and ospreys have opposable "thumbs" that make it easier to move their prey as they hold it. Many raptors have rough patches on the bottom of their feet. These provide increased friction that makes it harder for prey to squirm free.

Match the Raptor

There are approximately 482 species of raptor worldwide: 304 diurnal species and 178 nocturnal species. That sure makes identification tricky! Do you know which raptors are which?

American kestrel

great horned owl

bald eagle

peregrine falcon

1. Small and speedy, this raptor can fly more than twice as fast as a car drives on the highway! Adults grow up to 14-19 inches long (36-49 cm) with a wingspan of 3.3-3.6 feet (1-1.1m). They mostly eat other birds and catch their prey in mid-air. This wandering **falcon** can be found on every continent but Antarctica and lives in many different kinds of habitats. Some travel as many as 15,500 miles (25,000 km) in a single year!

2. This tiny **kestrel** is the smallest species of falcon in North America—only 4.7 to 10.6 inches long (12-27 cm). The males have blue-gray feathers on their wings, while the females are reddish-brown. Both the females and males have vertical stripes of black feathers near their eyes. They are predators who eat small animals like mice, lizards, and grasshoppers. Their small size means that even these tough predators are at risk of becoming prey to another, larger raptor.

3. The only **eagle** found exclusively in North America is both the national bird and the national animal for the United States of America. They are easily recognized by the bright, white feathers on their heads. This eagle can have a wingspan as large as 7.5 feet (2.3m)!

4. Feathery tufts on this **owl**'s head might look like ears, but they aren't. The ears are hidden in dark feathers on the sides of the bird's face. Their feathers are soft and make no rustling noises while the raptor is flying, allowing them to drop out of the sky onto unsuspecting prey. This nocturnal hunter sleeps during the day and tracks her prey at night.

Answers: 1-peregrine falcon, 2-American kestrel, 3-bald eagle, 4-great horned owl

Valuable Volunteers

Volunteers are very important in raptor centers. The veterinarians and rehabilitators rely on volunteers to:

- answer phone calls
- assist with releases
- carefully hold birds so that they don't get hurt when being examined, treated, or medicated
- clean cages
- educate the public
- exercise (fly) the raptors
- feed babies and adults
- raise money for these nonprofit centers
- transport birds to and from the center

What to do if you find a raptor in need

The best way to help a raptor in need is to call for help. Find a raptor center or licensed wildlife rehabilitator near you. You may also call US Fish and Wildlife Service (USFWS) or your state's Department of Natural Resources (DNR) or Department of Game, Fish, and Parks. All wild animals, even babies, can be dangerous. Raptors—with their powerful feet, sharp talons, and fierce beaks—do not understand that you want to help. They will try to defend themselves.

Do not try to take the raptor home or keep it as a pet. It is illegal to have raptors in captivity or to disturb nesting raptors without the proper permits from the State and Federal government.

To Kathy Woods, for equal parts inspiration, education, and laughter.—JKC

Thanks to the participating raptor centers and individuals for their photographs and for verifying the accuracy of the information in this book:

- California Raptor Center, UC Davis School of Veterinary Medicine, www.vetmed.ucdavis.edu/calraptor/index.cfm
- Carolina Raptor Center, www.carolinaraptorcenter.org
- Raptor Rehabilitation of Kentucky, www.raptorrehab.org
- Rocky Mountain Raptor Program, www.rmrp.org
- The Raptor Center at the University of Minnesota, www.raptor.cvm.umn.edu
- Tri-State Bird Rescue & Research, www.tristatebird.org
- Kathy Woods of the Phoenix Wildlife Center
- Peter McGowan of the U.S. Fish and Wildlife Service

Library of Congress Cataloging-in-Publication Data

Curtis, Jennifer Keats, author.
Raptor centers / by Jennifer Keats Curtis ; with California Raptor Center, UC Davis School of Veterinary Medicine, Carolina Raptor Center, Raptor Rehabilitation of Kentucky, Rocky Mountain Raptor Program, The Raptor Center at the University of Minnesota, Tri-State Bird Rescue & Research, and Peter McGowan of the U.S. Fish and Wildlife Service.
pages cm. -- (Animal helpers)
Other title: Animal helpers--raptor centers
Summary: "Even powerful birds of prey can get sick or hurt. When that happens, animal helpers at raptor centers come to the rescue! Dedicated staff treats injured, sick, and orphaned animals. They return the birds to their native environment or find forever homes at education and raptor centers for those that can't survive in the wild. Follow along in this photographic journal as staff and volunteers come together to care for these remarkable birds."-- Provided by publisher.
Audience: Ages 4-8.
ISBN 978-1-62855-447-2 (english hardcover : alk. paper) -- ISBN 978-1-62855-455-7 (english pbk. : alk. paper) -- ISBN 978-1-62855-471-7 (english downloadable ebook) -- ISBN 978-1-62855-487-8 (english interactive dual-language ebook) -- ISBN 978-1-62855-463-2 (spanish pbk. : alk. paper) -- ISBN 978-1-62855-479-3 (spanish downloadable ebook) -- ISBN 978-1-62855-495-3 (spanish interactive dual-language ebook) 1. Birds of prey--Wounds and injuries--Treatment--Juvenile literature. 2. Wildlife rehabilitation--Juvenile literature. 3. Wildlife rescue--Juvenile literature. I. Title. II. Title: Animal helpers--raptor centers. III. Series: Curtis, Jennifer Keats. Animal helpers.

QL677.78.C88 2014
639.97'89--dc23

2014011054

Translated into Spanish: Ayudantes de animales: Centros de aves rapaces

Lexile® Level: 880
key phrases for educators: adaptations, Environmental Education, helping animals, jobs, raptors

Bibliography

In addition to the above-listed raptor centers that participated in this book, the author has consulted the following resources:

BirdLife Data Zone. Accessed January 24, 2014. <http://www.birdlife.org/datazone/home>.

Blair, Sharon K. "Caring for Raptors (Birds of Prey)." Bird Care & Conservation Society. Revised July 2000. <http://www.birdcare.asn.au/pdf/raptors.pdf>.

Collard, Sneed B. *Birds of Prey: A Look at Daytime Raptors*. New York: Watts Library, 1999.

Global Raptor Information Network. Accessed February 13, 2014. <http://globalraptors.org>.

IUCN Red List of Threatened Species. International Union for Conservation of Nature and Natural Resources. Accessed January 27, 2014. <http://www.iucnredlist.org>.

Laubach, Christyna M., René Laubach, and Charles W.G. Smith. *Raptor! A Kid's Guide to Birds of Prey*. Boston, MA: Storey Publishing, 2002.

Phoenix Wildlife Center. Accessed February 1, 2014. <http://phoenixwildlifecenter.net>.

"Raptors of the World." Raptor Research Foundation. Accessed January 15, 2014. <http://www.raptorresearchfoundation.org/education/raptor-world>.

Printed in China, December 2018
This product conforms to CPSIA 2008
Second Printing

Arbordale Publishing
Mt. Pleasant, SC 29464
www.ArbordalePublishing.com